Railways & Recollections

1965

Contents

First published in 2011

British Library Cataloguing in Publication Data
A catalogue record for this book is available from the British Library.

Printed and bound in Česká Republika

ISBN 978 1 85794 376 4

Silver Link Publishing Ltd
The Trundle
Ringstead Road
Great Addington
Kettering
Northants NN14 4BW
Tel/Fax: 01536 330588
email: sales@nostalgiacollection.com
Website: www.nostalgiacollection.com

Title page: **BOURNEMOUTH:** Nine Elms driver Joe McCarthy stands proudly beside No 34059 *Sir Archibald Sinclair*, which he has just driven from Waterloo at the head of the 14.13 express on Saturday 25 July. This photograph helps illustrate the scale of a big express locomotive – in this case a 4-6-2 'West Country' Class 'light Pacific', designed by the Southern Railway's CME Oliver Bulleid and built at Brighton Works in April 1947.

This locomotive was withdrawn less than a year later, in May 1966, but unlike most of its stablemates it escaped the cutter's torch and was preserved by the Bulleid Society. It can still be seen today, restored and in action on the Bluebell Railway, Sussex, where you too can stand alongside those mighty 6ft 2in driving wheels at the platform and marvel at the 86 tons of raw power towering above you.

Acknowledgements

First and foremost we would like to record our gratitude to the late Ray Ruffell, without whose efforts to photograph and record the railway scene in 1965 this book would not have been possible.

Introduction

The year is 1965 and it is a year of great change. Swinging Britain is indeed in full swing, with its music and fashion sweeping across the globe. On London's Carnaby Street, skirts are getting shorter, and the Beatles spend a total of 13 weeks at No 1 in the singles chart. But the biggest-selling record of 1965 is Ken Dodd's *Tears*, which spent five weeks at No 1 and outsold all the Fab Four's offerings put together!

Yet, slowly, the old order was disappearing. This was the year that Britain abolished the death penalty, and it was also the year that Britain's great wartime leader, Sir Winston Churchill, passed away, at the age of 90. He had stood down as a backbench MP less than a year earlier. His body lay in state for three days and a state funeral service was held at St Paul's Cathedral in London, attended by the Queen and the largest-ever gathering of past and present world leaders. His lead-lined coffin was then taken by boat along the River Thames, where dockers lowered their crane jibs in an impromptu salute.

As the Royal Artillery fired a 19-gun salute and the RAF staged a flypast of 16 aircraft, Churchill's body was taken to Waterloo station, where it was loaded onto a specially prepared carriage for its final journey to the family plot at St Martin's Church, Bladon, in Oxfordshire. The funeral train of Pullman coaches carrying the mourners was hauled by the steam locomotive named in his honour – No 34051 *Winston Churchill*.

The locomotive *Winston Churchill* is, appropriately, a 'Battle of Britain' class 'light Pacific', built in December 1946. It was retired from active service later in 1965 and today is a static exhibit at the National Railway Museum in York. It was designed by Oliver Bulleid, the brilliant Southern Railway Chief Mechanical Engineer (CME), who came up with some brilliant locomotive designs to solve the Southern's chronic traction shortage during the dark days of the Second World War.

But even Bulleid's reputation was overshadowed by another great man who passed away in 1965. Sir William Stanier, the legendary locomotive designer of the London, Midland & Scottish Railway (LMS), who created some of the greatest steam machines ever. He will be best remembered for the powerful 'Princess Royal' and 'Princess Coronation' classes of express locomotives that famously plied the West Coast Main Line from London to the North, yet he also had a talent for creating brilliant workhorses too, like the 'Black Five' mixed-traffic 4-6-0 and the 8F 2-8-0 heavy goods locomotive.

However, in 1965 the steam locomotive designer's art was a forgotten one. The rich variety of surviving steam engines on the British Railways roster – some dating back to the Victorian era – was rapidly diminishing, to be replaced by modern diesel and electric locomotives. This was the era of new technology – described as 'the white heat of

technology' by British Prime Minister Harold Wilson – and that meant building spacecraft. The so-called space race was being run by the USSR and the USA, and 1965 saw both the competing superpowers set up space walks.

The Second World War had ended two decades earlier, but now a new conflict was claiming lives. This was the year that the USA made the fateful decision to send in troops to prevent South Vietnam falling to the communist North Vietnam. By the time America pulled out 18 years later, 58,220 US troops had been killed in the conflict, together with an estimated 2 million Vietnamese soldiers and civilians.

1965 was the year musician Bob Dylan upset acoustic folk fans by playing an electric guitar. But he more than anyone could have told them that the times they were a-changin'. The world was moving on.

Happily, most of the UK's superb railway network was still intact, as the Beeching cuts were yet to bite. Branch-line Britain still existed as a very real place where small country stations were more famous for their immaculate flower displays than their passenger numbers. And impressive steam engines still roared through most parts of the country, hauling express passenger trains and clanking collections of assorted freight wagons.

It was this scene that photographer-railwayman Ray Ruffell set out to record with his camera, before it was too late. And in doing so he succeeded in capturing a Britain that's gone but never forgotten.

1965 Happenings (1)

January
- The Prime Minister of Northern Ireland and the Taoiseach of the Republic of Ireland meet for the first time in 43 years.
- Sir Winston Churchill dies on the 24th. His state funeral follows six days later, attended by the largest-ever gathering of world statesmen.

February
- Stanley Matthews plays his final First Division football match, aged 50yrs 5days!
- Canada gets a new flag – the red and white maple-leaf design.
- Gambia gains independence from the UK.

March
- The first American combat troops – 3,500 Marines – arrive in South Vietnam.
- Goldie, a London Zoo golden eagle, is recaptured 12 days after her escape.
- Russian cosmonaut Aleksei Leonov becomes the first person to walk in space.
- Luxembourg wins the Eurovision Song Contest with *Poupée de Cire, Poupée de Son*, sung by France Gall (music and lyrics by Serge Gainsbourg).

April
- *My Fair Lady* wins eight Academy Awards, including Best Picture and Best Director, while *Mary Poppins* takes home five Oscars. Julie Andrews wins an Academy Award for Best Actress.
- The first protest march against the Vietnam War draws 25,000 protestors to Washington.

Men and machines

CHILWORTH: It wasn't all glamour on the footplate of a steam locomotive. It was hard, dirty and physical work – sweltering hot in summer and often bitterly cold in winter. We're on 'U' Class 2-6-0 No 31639 at the head of

READING: Same engine, different faces. Here's 'U' Class No 31639 again, this time pausing at Reading New Junction with local driver Whitbread and fireman Stagg posing with their machine. No 31639 was one of 50 of these mixed-traffic 2-6-0 'Moguls' designed by

Richard Maunsell and built between 1928 and 1931. The entire class was withdrawn between 1962 and 1966 and most – including this one – were scrapped. There are, however, four that survived into preservation, two on the Bluebell Railway and two on the Mid-Hants Railway.

the Blisworth to Redhill parcels train on 4 September, with Guildford driver B. Heath and fireman A. Earle nursing the engine up the steep Shere Heath Bank between Chilworth and Comshall.

Right **SOUTHAMPTON:** 'Merchant Navy' Class 4-6-2 No 35003 *Royal Mail* takes on water at Southampton, en route to Bournemouth from Waterloo hauling the 'Bournemouth Belle' Pullman service on 19 January. Bournemouth driver Ray Foyle and an unknown fireman are topping up the tender's water tank, which had an impressive capacity of 6,000 gallons. *Royal Mail* was the third of its class to be built, in September 1941, and was among the last to be withdrawn, in July 1967. Holder of the class speed record of almost 106mph, it was also the last steam locomotive to achieve an authenticated 100mph on British Railways. Such a shame that this historic engine was scrapped.

Below **WIMBLEDON:** An unnamed driver pauses for the photographer at the controls of 'S15' Class 4-6-0 No 30838 at Wimbledon West Yard on 6 January. He has just worked a milk tank and brake-van from Clapham Yard, via Earlsfield.

The 'S15' freight engine was designed by Robert Urie for the London & South Western Railway (LSWR) in 1920 and, after the LSWR was absorbed into the Southern Railway at the Grouping of 1923, continued to be produced by the SR until 1936 (the later ones with modifications by the SR's CME, Richard Maunsell). A total of 45 were built at Eastleigh Works and the class continued in service through to 1966, when the last examples were withdrawn. Seven have been preserved, but not alas No 30838.

Right **CROWTHORNE:** It was getting near the end of the line for all British steam locomotives in 1965, so dedicated railway enthusiasts decided to make the most of what was left by chartering special trains, hauled by their favourite locomotives. Here, on Sunday 3 January, is 'N' Class 2-6-0 No 31831 heading the 'Maunsell Commemorative Railtour', organised by the Locomotive Club of Great Britain, near Crowthorne, en route from Reading to Redhill. Maunsell designed the 'N' Class in 1914 for mixed-traffic duties on the South Eastern & Chatham Railway (SECR) and 80 were built, including 15 by the Southern between 1932 and 1934. All were withdrawn by 1966 and only one was preserved, No 31874, on the Mid-Hants Railway.

Left **WATERLOO:** Driver Joe Langdon of Bournemouth is on the footplate of a member of the 'Merchant Navy' Class of 'Pacifics' – No 35003 *Royal Mail* – which is again about to depart with the 'Bournemouth Belle'.

1965 Happenings (2)

May
- The Pennine Way long-distance footbath officially opens.
- Liverpool wins the FA Cup Final, beating Leeds Utd 2-1.
- Muhammad Ali knocks out Sonny Liston in the first round of their Heavyweight Championship rematch.

June
- Astronaut Edward Higgins White makes the first US space walk.

July
- The Mont Blanc Tunnel is opened.
- Bob Dylan upsets folk purists by 'going electric' at the Newport Folk Festival.
- Edward Heath becomes Leader of the British Conservative Party.
- President Lyndon B. Johnson increases the number of US troops in South Vietnam from 75,000 to 125,000.
- Cigarette advertising is banned on British television.

August
- The Beatles perform at Shea Stadium in New York.

September
- Hurricane Betsy strikes Louisiana with winds of 145mph, causing 76 deaths and $1.42 billion of damage.
- The world's biggest tanker, *Tokyo Maru*, is launched in Japan.

Above **SOUTHAMPTON:** And here is *Royal Mail* yet again hauling the 'Bournemouth Belle' – this time at Southampton Central – with driver Ray Foyle about to set off for the last leg of the journey from Waterloo to the Dorset seaside resort.

Left **READING:** It's 2 January and driver Boyce, fireman Ashey and guard Eric Marshall, all from Guildford, are about to depart on the 23.10 from Reading Southern to Guildford. Why the special group photograph? It's because this is the very last steam-hauled passenger service between the two stations.

WOKINGHAM: Here's driver Boyce on that last train, between Wokingham and Crowthorne, at the controls of 'Standard 4' 2-6-0 No 76059.

Left **GUILDFORD:** Fireman Jack Ward and an unnamed driver pose on the last train into Guildford that evening, the 22.18, hauled by the same locomotive.

Below left **READING:** Another photograph taken on that day at Reading Southern shows this time driver Bob Ward and foreman Peter Painter on the 17.47 train about to set off for Redhill, hauled by 'U' Class 2-6-0 No 31627. Reading Southern, a terminus that adjoined the former GWR's Reading General Station, was closed later that year, with its trains diverted to the latter.

Out and about

Below **WEYMOUTH:** This is what a typical loco yard looked like in the latter years of steam on British Rail. Here's Weymouth's North Yard on 3 February – a wonderfully grimy collection of heavy lifting gear, ramshackle buildings (including a grounded coach body for the staff's mess room), and a couple of very different steam locomotives. In the background is 'West Country' Class 'Pacific' No 34013 *Okehampton*, which was built at Brighton Works in 1945 and continued in service until July 1967, when it was scrapped. In the foreground is No 41261, a Class 2 2-6-2 tank engine, one of 130 built to the design of the LMS's CME George Ivatt in 1946.

WATERLOO: We're back at the Southern Region's magnificent London terminus on 1 February, with two express trains waiting to depart. On the left is the 10.45 'Canberra' express, hauled by 'West Country' Class No 34103 *Calstock*. To the right is 'Battle of Britain' Class 4-6-2 No 34089 *602 Squadron* at the head of the 10.30 for Weymouth. The two locomotives have a lot in common – both were 'light Pacifics' designed by Oliver Bulleid, *602 Squadron* was built at Eastleigh, entered service in December 1948 and was withdrawn in July 1967, while *Calstock* was built at Brighton in 1950 and retired in September 1965. Both were scrapped.

GUILDFORD: Here's another 'West Country' 'Pacific', simmering gently at Guildford on 16 February. This is No 34032 *Camelford*, built at Brighton in 1946 and scrapped just 20 months after this photograph was taken. The affection the old crews had for their locomotives is legendary – note the affectionate nickname 'Superheat Sid' chalked on the smokebox door.

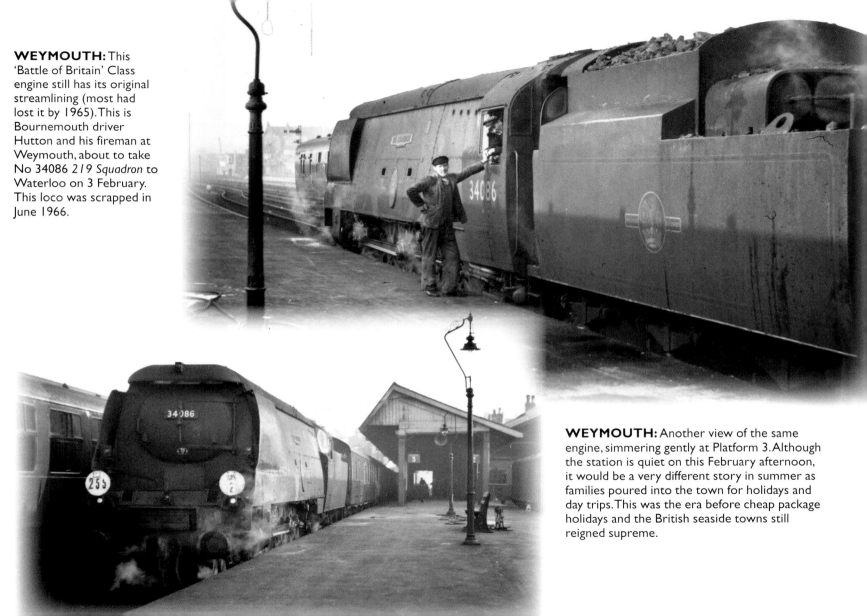

WEYMOUTH: This 'Battle of Britain' Class engine still has its original streamlining (most had lost it by 1965). This is Bournemouth driver Hutton and his fireman at Weymouth, about to take No 34086 *219 Squadron* to Waterloo on 3 February. This loco was scrapped in June 1966.

WEYMOUTH: Another view of the same engine, simmering gently at Platform 3. Although the station is quiet on this February afternoon, it would be a very different story in summer as families poured into the town for holidays and day trips. This was the era before cheap package holidays and the British seaside towns still reigned supreme.

Below **SANDHURST:** Summer is still a long way off on 5 March, with residents of Surrey waking up to a blanket of snow following a 15-hour blizzard. 'U' Class 2-6-0 No 31800 passes Little Sandhurst Bridge on the early Guildford to Reading freight.

Above **CROWTHORNE:** On the same morning the 10.24 passenger service from Reading to Tonbridge braves the drifts at Crowthorne.

Right **AMBARROW HILL:** You didn't have to worry about 'the wrong kind of snow' bringing the railways to a halt back in 1965 – they just kept running! Here's another 'U' Class 2-6-0, this time No 31791, climbing up past Ambarrow Hill between Sandhurst and Crowthorne with the 09.00 Guildford-Reading freight, also on 5 March.

Below **HAVANT:** 'Battle of Britain' 4-6-2 No 34077 *603 Squadron* storms past Havant at the head of a Brighton to Plymouth express on the morning of 2 March. This locomotive was built at Brighton, entered service in July 1948 and was scrapped in March 1967.

GUILDFORD: Here's a lovely view of 'N' Class 2-6-0 No 31811 outside Guildford engine shed on 9 March. This workhorse class of locomotive had been around since the First World War, but its days were numbered.

1966 Happenings (3)

October
- Police find the body of 10-year-old Lesley Ann Downey on Saddleworth Moor, Lancashire. Ian Brady and his 23-year-old girlfriend Myra Hindley are arrested.
- A fortnight later, Brady and Hindley appear in court, charged with the murder of Lesley Ann Downey as well as Edward Evans, 17, and John Kilbride, 12.

November
- A trolleybus plunges into the Nile at Cairo, killing 74 passengers.
- The death penalty is abolished in the UK.
- Craig Breedlove sets a new land speed record of 600.601mph.

December
- The Beatles release their *Rubber Soul* album.
- A 70mph speed limit is imposed on Britain's roads.
- David Lean's film of *Doctor Zhivago*, starring Omar Sharif and Julie Christie, is released in the UK.
- The British oil platform *Sea Gem* collapses in the North Sea.

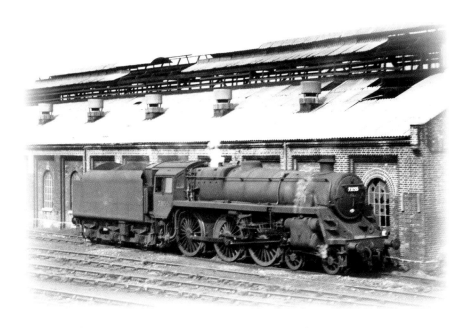

Above right **READING:** Another engine shed, another locomotive – this time 'Standard 5' 4-6-0 No 73155 at Reading Southern Shed on 3 April. This was one of 172 built by BR between 1951 and 1957, based very much on the highly successful 'Black Five', designed by Sir William Stanier, who was to die later this year, aged 89.

Right **GUILDFORD:** 'N' Class 2-6-0 No 31408 has a full tender of coal following its visit to Guildford's coal stage on 14 April. Waiting its turn in the background is 'Q1' Class 0-6-0 No 33009.

Southern delights

Below **EASTLEIGH:** A famous named passenger service of the era was the 'Pines Express', which ran between Manchester and Bournemouth. Here it is rushing through Eastleigh on 30 April, headed by 'West Country' Class 4-6-2 No 34040 *Crewkerne*, which was built at Brighton in 1946 and scrapped in July 1967. The 'Pines Express' ran between 1910 and 1967 and is believed to have been named after the pine trees on the outskirts of Bournemouth that greeted visitors to the Dorset seaside resort. It was the most famous express to use the much-loved scenic Somerset & Dorset Joint Railway, but after 1962 it was diverted via Oxford, Reading, Basingstoke and Southampton. Later this year, the service would be extended to neighbouring Poole, but its days were numbered and the final 'Pines' ran on 4 March 1967.

Above right **SHEPTON MALLET:** By 1965 the days of the Somerset & Dorset Joint Railway were numbered – it was scheduled to close in 1966 – so enthusiasts made the most of the time remaining by regularly chartering special excursions. On 4 April the 'Wessex Downsman' was one such train, pictured here crossing Shepton Mallet viaduct. At the head of the train is 8F 2-8-0 No 48309.

MIDFORD: The same train is now rounding a curve near Midford station – a single-platform halt on the Bath extension of the S&DR, near where the double-track line became a single track. The station was axed with the rest of the line in March 1966. With a fine exhaust plume at the head of the train, No 48309 is making light work of hauling the 13 packed coaches – and no wonder. The 8F was another famous locomotive designed by Sir William Stanier for the LMS, this time for heavy freight, and 852 were built between 1935 and 1946. Many survived until the end of steam in 1968.

Below **EARLSFIELD:** 'Merchant Navy' Class 4-6-2 No 35023 *Holland-Afrika Line* heads the heavy 13.30 Waterloo to Bournemouth and Weymouth express near Earlsfield on 21 April. Note the third rail for the electric commuter trains that shared this line.

Right **READING:** Another golden oldie – 'N' Class 2-6-0 No 31858 at Reading SR shed on 8 May, still steaming after all those years.

1966 ARRIVALS AND DEPARTURES

BIRTHS

Vinnie Jones	Footballer and actor	5 January
Joely Richardson	Actress	9 January
Hugh Fearnley-Whittingstall	TV chef	14 January
James Nesbitt	Actor	15 January
Sophie	Countess of Wessex	20 January
Michael Dell	Computer manufacturer	23 February
Lawrence Llewelyn-Bowen	Designer and TV presenter	11 March
Robert Downey Jr	Actor	4 April
Norman Whiteside	Footballer	7 May
Linda Evangelista	Supermodel	10 May
Brooke Shields	Actress	31 May
Damien Hirst	Artist	7 June
Elizabeth Hurley	Model and actress	10 June
Jo Whiley	Radio presenter	4 July
J. K. Rowling	'Harry Potter' author	31 July
Shania Twain	Country singer	28 August
Lennox Lewis	Boxer	2 September
Charlie Sheen	Actor	3 September
Steve Coogan	Comedian and actor	14 October
Björk	Icelandic singer	21 November

Farouk I	King of Egypt	(b1920)	18 March
Sonny Boy Williamson	Blues musician	(b1899)	25 May
Wally Hammond	England cricketer	(b1903)	1 July
Albert Schweitzer	Missionary	(b1875)	4 September
Sir William Stanier	Locomotive engineer	(b1876)	27 September
Clara Bow	Silent film actress	(b1905)	27 September
W. Somerset Maugham	Writer	(b1874)	16 December
Richard Dimbleby	Broadcaster	(b1913)	22 December

DEATHS

T. S. Eliot	Poet and dramatist	(b1888)	4 January
Winston Churchill	Former Prime Minister	(b1874)	24 January
Nat King Cole	Musician	(b1919)	15 February
Malcolm X	American political activist (assassinated)	(b1925)	21 February
Stan Laurel	British-born comedy actor	(b1890)	23 February

Left **GUILDFORD:** Although the 'Q1' was designed for hauling freight, it was much loved by railway enthusiasts – hence one was chartered for the Railway Enthusiasts Club's special last train from Guildford to Horsham on 12 June. This is No 33006, which, like all but one in its class, was destined to be scrapped at the end of steam on British Rail.

Below **NEAR WATERLOO:** 'Battle of Britain' Class 4-6-2 No 34064 *Fighter Command* has just left Waterloo and is already building up speed as it heads for Vauxhall at the head of the 10.54 express to Salisbury on 12 June.

Raw power

Left **GUILDFORD:** On 27 May at Guildford are two very different engines, designed by the same man. The Southern Railway's CME Oliver Bulleid was responsible for the 'West Country' 'light Pacific' express locomotives (left) and the 'Q1' 0-6-0 freight engines (right). The latter was the most powerful 0-6-0 steam loco ever built, and its distinctive appearance was down to its austere wartime build – 40 were produced in 1940 to help with the war effort. The express engine is No 34015 *Exmouth*, built in 1945 and scrapped in 1967.

CLAPHAM JUNCTION: 'Q1' No 33009 demonstrates why it gained its reputation for being the most powerful 0-6-0 ever built as it passes Clapham 'A' Box with a heavy freight train from Nine Elms to Feltham on 12 June.

Opposite **BAYNARDS:** Still on the subject of those wonderful 'Q1s', here are a brace of the 0-6-0s – Nos 33027 and 33006 – at Baynards on the Locomotive Club of Great Britain's 'Wealdsman' rail tour on 13 June.

HEATHFIELD: It wasn't just 'Q1s' that took starring roles on the 'Wealdsman' rail tour. Here are 2-6-0s Nos 31803 and 31411 drawing an appreciative crowd of enthusiasts, who were free to roam the tracks in those far-off days before Health & Safety came to rule our lives...

FOREST ROW: The 'Wealdsman' tour is seen again, double-headed by Nos 31803 and 31411.

Heading north

CREWE: Our photographer Ray Ruffell got away to other parts of the country as often as possible to photograph the final years of steam on British Rail. On 15 June he headed north through former LMS territory and managed to snatch this atmospheric shot of Crewe South shed as he passed by on the Euston-Crewe express. At the time this photograph was taken South shed had received an influx of extra locomotives following the decision to close the nearby Crewe North shed. Countless examples can be seen here, simmering away gently – a sight we'll never see the like of again.

1965 No 1 Records (1)

January
I Feel Fine — Beatles
Yeh Yeh — Georgie Fame & The Blue Flames
Go Now — Moody Blues

February
You've Lost That Loving Feeling — Righteous Brothers
Tired of Waiting — Kinks
I'll Never Find Another You — Seekers

March
It's Not Unusual — Tom Jones
The Last Time — Rolling Stones

April
Concrete and Clay — Unit Four Plus Two
The Minute You've Gone — Cliff Richard
Ticket to Ride — Beatles

May
King of the Road — Roger Miller
Where Are You Now (My Love) — Jackie Trent
Long Live Love — Sandie Shaw

June
Crying In The Chapel — Elvis Presley
I'm Alive — Hollies

July
Mr Tambourine Man — Byrds

LLANDUDNO: A day later Ray took this photograph of Llandudno Junction from his passing train. There's a tantalising glimpse of the engine shed, with at least three tank engines standing outside, as well as the coal stage.

Opposite top **LOCH CARRON:** It's 23 June and we're on the Kyle of Lochalsh line, alongside Loch Carron, a sea loch on the west coast of Ross & Cromarty in the Scottish Highlands.

Above **BANGOR:** Cement wagons dominate the sidings at Bangor on 17 June, but the eye is drawn to ex-LMS Class 2 2-6-2T No 41200.

Right **ALVES:** Here's another of Ray's photos from a moving train, this time much further north, on 21 June. A diesel shunter is hauling the local freight on the Burghead and Hopeman branch, near Alves. Ray was travelling on the Inverness-Aberdeen express.

WICK: This is almost as far north as you can travel by train on the British mainland. Sadly, on 24 June 1965 Wick station is dominated by diesels. On the left, D5329 is at the head of a parcels train, while on the right D5126 is ready to leave with the 17.00 passenger train to Inverness.

WOKINGHAM: As 1965 draws to a close, electric and diesel traction is steadily replacing the beloved steam locomotives of British Rail, but the transformation of the network wasn't without its teething problems. The railwaymen brought up on steam power had a wry laugh whenever the new engines failed. This scene on the evening of 13 December must have raised plenty of chuckles in the mess room as 'U' Class 2-6-0 No 31803 arrives at Wokingham after pushing failed 'Tadpole' unit No 1206 from Sandhurst…

Up the Junction

CLAPHAM JUNCTION: Back on Southern Region rails, 'West Country' Class No 34036 *Westward Ho!* heads the 11.30 express from Waterloo to Bournemouth and Weymouth past Clapham Junction – the busiest station in the UK, thanks to the fact that trains from Waterloo and Victoria are funnelled through it. Even today more than 2,000 trains a day pass through.

As an aside, did you know that Clapham Junction isn't actually in Clapham – it's in Battersea? That's because when the station was opened in 1863 Battersea was regarded as a downmarket district of London, while Clapham, a mile to the east, was seen as more fashionable. The name has stuck ever since.

Moreover, Clapham is without doubt the only junction in the world that has been the subject of a book, play, film and two songs. *Up the Junction* was a 1963 novel written by Nell Dunn, depicting life in the slums around the station. In 1965 it was adapted for BBC television, and in 1968 a film version starring Susan George, Dennis Waterman and Maureen Lipman was released. Meanwhile, 1960s pop group Manfred Mann produced the soundtrack, which included a single *Up the Junction*. Later, in 1979, the post-punk band Squeeze released another song with the same title, about the unplanned pregnancy of a 'girl from Clapham'; it reached No 2 in the UK singles chart.

RAYNES PARK: 'Merchant Navy' Class 4-6-2 No 35028 *Clan Line* is pictured between Raynes Park and New Malden on 29 July, heading the 'Royal Wessex' express. *Clan Line* entered service in December 1948 and was operational until July 1967. It was one of the few steam locomotives saved from the scrapyard and is today operational and main-line certified. It is maintained at Stewarts Lane depot, London, which until 1962 was one of the biggest motive power depots in the country.

Below left **EASTLEIGH:** 'Battle of Britain' Class 4-6-2 No 34064 *Fighter Command* rushes through Eastleigh on a relief Waterloo to Bournemouth express. Built at Brighton Works in 1947, it was withdrawn in May 1966. Interestingly, this was the only British Rail locomotive in its class fitted with a Giesl ejector – a suction draught system invented in 1951 by the Austrian engineer Dr Adolph Giesl-Gieslingen. The Giesl ejector was designed to improve suction draught, with the existing blastpipe replaced by several smaller diverging blastpipes. Giesl claimed that his ejector enabled the locomotive to use up to 12 per cent less coal and increased power by up to 20 per cent. The crews that manned No 34064 were suitably impressed and demonstrated that it did indeed 'do what it said on the tin', but with the end of steam in sight BR only fitted the Giesl ejector to one more of its diminishing fleet of steam locomotives – a BR Class 9F 2-10-0 freight engine. However, in the 1980s the Keighley & Worth Valley Railway fitted a Giesl ejector to its own Bulleid 'light Pacific' – preserved 'West Country' Class No 34092 *City of Wells* – which is currently undergoing an overhaul at the West Yorkshire heritage line.

Below right **WOKINGHAM:** 'U' Class 2-6-0 No 31803 arrives at Wokingham on the 17.08 passenger service from Reading on 19 July. Designed by the Southern Railway's CME, Richard Maunsell, 50 'U' Class locomotives were built between 1928 and 1931. By 1965 these workhorse 'Moguls' were becoming an uncommon sight, as they were being replaced by demoted 'West Country' and 'Battle of Britain' Class 'light Pacifics' for branch-line work.

Below **WOKINGHAM:** 'N' Class 2-6-0 No 31816 shunts Wokingham up yard on 24 July. Back in 1965 Britain's coal was shifted around the country by rail and most coal merchants were based in railway yards. The local coalman can be seen in the middle distance, loading his truck with sacks of the black stuff that still heated most homes in those days. The distinctive spire in the background of the photograph belongs to St Paul's Church, Wokingham. It looks several centuries old, but in fact wasn't built until 1864, contributed by local patron John Walter at his own expense. It was consecrated by the Bishop of Oxford on 23 July 1864 – exactly 99 years and one day before this photograph was taken! By contrast, Wokingham station is a much older affair – it was built in 1849 when the Reading to Farnborough line reached the town.

Above **GUILDFORD:** When Britain's wartime leader Sir Winston Churchill passed away in January this year, the 'Battle of Britain' Class 'light Pacific' No 34051 *Winston Churchill* was the obvious choice to haul his funeral train from London to Oxfordshire. It was still in service when this photograph was taken at Guildford on 13 July, but not for long – it was withdrawn in September, and later became a static exhibit at the National Railway Museum in York.

Below **SOUTHAMPTON:** This is Southampton Old Docks on 20 July, with 'West Country' Class 4-6-2 No 34097 *Holsworthy* off the 'Northern Star' boat train. In the background is USA-built 0-6-0T docks shunter No 30067.

Above **EFFINGHAM JUNCTION:** It's 13 December at Effingham Junction, and a typical busy scene, with Standard Class 5 4-6-0 No 73155 on the down road and 4 SUB electric unit No 4164 about to set off for Waterloo via Epsom. Driver Stockton from Nine Elms is standing in the staffroom doorway.

WIMBLEDON: What a fine exhaust as 'West Country' Class No 34024 *Tamar Valley* sweeps through Wimbledon with the 13.30 express from Waterloo to Bournemouth and Weymouth on 13 August. This locomotive was built at Brighton in 1946 and rebuilt in 1961, but withdrawn in July 1967.

WATERLOO: How I remember watching in excitement the great Bulleid 'Pacifics' when I visited Waterloo station as a child, en route to Hampshire for family holidays in the New Forest. I may even have been here on this day, 12 August, as 'Merchant Navy' Class 4-6-2 No 35026 *Lamport & Holt Line* backs out of the terminus after working in on an express from Weymouth. However, as a nine-year-old I would have been on the platform looking up in wonder at the unforgettable steam giants, while photographer Ray was looking down from the window of Waterloo's guards' room when he snapped this shot of a great engine that would be scrapped just 18 months later.

Isle of Wight

RYDE ST JOHN'S ROAD: With the Isle of Wight and its unique steam railway just a short hop across the Solent, Ray was a regular visitor to the island. On 5 August he was enjoying a ride on the Cowes to Ryde train when he took this photograph of Class 'O2' 0-4-4T tank engine No 27 *Merstone* under repair at Ryde St John's Road. This engine was built by the LSWR at Nine Elms in 1890 and, after the Grouping of 1923, was cascaded down to the Isle of Wight Railway in 1926, where it remained until withdrawn in 1967. Although it was scrapped, its stablemate No W24 *Calbourne* (built a year later and sent to the island a year earlier) is preserved and still runs on the heritage Isle of Wight Steam Railway.

HAVENSTREET: The Cowes to Ryde train coasts into the platform at Havenstreet, while its opposite number heading back to Ryde awaits departure at the platform, headed by No 33 *Bembridge*, another 0-4-4T ex-LSWR tank engine. This one was built at Nine Elms in 1892 and moved to the Isle of Wight in 1928. It was withdrawn later this year and, unfortunately, scrapped.

More Southern delights

Above **BOURNEMOUTH:** The famous 'Bournemouth Belle' Pullman express arrives at the resort from Waterloo on 29 August, passing over the viaduct between Bournemouth West Junction and Gasworks Junction.

Right **SANDHURST:** 'Standard 4' 2-6-0 No 76033 is about to leave Sandhurst Halt at 17.08 on 17 August with a Reading to Redhill passenger service.

Below **BOURNEMOUTH:** On the same day at Bournemouth West, the 09.30 express from Waterloo has arrived, hauled by 'West Country' Class 4-6-2 No 34046 *Braunton*. This locomotive, built at Brighton in 1946, was withdrawn just three months after this photograph was taken, in October 1965, but unlike most other engines was spared the cutter's torch. Today it is privately owned and operated by the West Somerset Railway Association.

Above **SOUTHAMPTON:** Photographer Ray stood on the roof of the Southampton Ocean Terminal to capture this image of 'West Country' Class 4-6-2 No 34033 *Chard* arriving on 19 August. This locomotive was scrapped in December 1965, just 19 years after it was built. Note the parked cars, which are mainly British-built, with the exception of a brace of VW 'Beetles'.

Above **FARNBOROUGH:**
A commuter express to Waterloo arrives at Farnborough at 07.35 on 3 August, hauled by BR Standard Class 5 4-6-0 No 73043.

Right **BOURNEMOUTH:**
This is Bournemouth West station on 29 August. Again the eye is drawn to the car park and the magnificent array of saloons – and all British!

Right **REDHILL:** This is the view from the footplate as 'U' Class 2-6-0 No 31639 runs into Redhill with the Blisworth Parcels on 4 September.

Below **VAUXHALL:** There's something incongruous about the juxtapositioning of a steam locomotive and 1960s glass and steel office blocks and flats, but that's what a bystander at Vauxhall would have seen on 16 September as the 11.30 Waterloo to Bournemouth and Weymouth, hauled by 'Battle of Britain' Class 4-6-2 No 34071 *601 Squadron,* roared (or should that be flew?) past.

Below right **EGHAM:** The 08.53 Bournemouth to Waterloo service has been diverted through Egham on 28 November. It is headed by 'Merchant Navy' Class 4-6-2 No 35013 *Blue Funnel,* which entered service in February 1945 and was scrapped in July 1967.

CLAPHAM JUNCTION: Here we are again on one of the 17 platforms at Britain's busiest railway station. As many as 200 trains an hour could pass through here at peak times, but now it's 11.42 on 16 September and things are quieter as BR Standard Class 3 2-6-2T engines Nos 82018 and 82028 go about their duties. There were 45 locomotives in this class, all built at Swindon Works between April 1952 and August 1955 to a design by Robert Riddles that was based on the chassis of the LMS Ivatt Class 4 with a GWR boiler bolted on. Designed to last for 40 years, the actual working life of these engines was woefully short – one was only in service for eight years – and they were all withdrawn between 1964 and 1967, and all scrapped.

Above **WOKINGHAM:** Now here's a truly rare sight on Southern metals – *Flying Scotsman* with LNER livery and number (4472) passing through Wokingham on a Locomotive Club of Great Britain rail tour from Waterloo to Derby.

Probably the most famous locomotive in history, LNER Class 'A3' 'Pacific' No 4472 *Flying Scotsman* was built in 1923 at Doncaster Works to the design of the legendary engineer, Nigel Gresley. It was one of five Gresley 'Pacifics' chosen to haul the prestigious non-stop 'Flying Scotsman' service from London to Edinburgh, running an eight-wheel tender with a capacity of 9 tons of coal, which enabled the train to travel the 392 miles in 8 hours non-stop. The tender included a corridor to allow crews to change over without stopping the train. On 30 November 1934 it was the first steam loco to be officially recorded at 100mph. It remained in service with British Railways until January 1963, when it was sold into private ownership. Its new owner, Alan Pegler, had it restored to LNER condition, which is how it is seen here.

After a colourful life in preservation, during which it was bought by a succession of owners, including music producer and railway enthusiast Pete Waterman, it was bought in 2004 by the National Railway Museum in York. It is estimated that it has covered more than 2 million miles in its lifetime.

Below **REDHILL:** Fireman Earle and driver Heath of Guildford turn 'U' Class No 31639 on the turntable at Redhill, after working in on the Blisworth Parcels.

1965 No 1 Records (2)

August
Help!   Beatles
I Got You Babe   Sonny & Cher

September
Satisfaction   Rolling Stones
Make It Easy On Yourself   Walker Brothers
Tears   Ken Dodd

November
Get Off Of My Cloud   Rolling Stones
The Carnival Is Over   Seekers

December
Day Tripper   Beatles

WATERLOO: Anybody who travelled to or from Waterloo in the 1960s will feel a warm glow of nostalgia as they see this evocative view through the gates to Platform 16, where the 08.34 from Bournemouth has just arrived behind Standard Class 5 No 73118.

Above **WATERLOO:** 'West Country' Class 'light Pacific' No 34044 *Woolacombe* is about to leave London on 3 October at the head of the Greek Line 'Arcadia' boat train.

Above **BOURNEMOUTH:** Ray climbed to the top of an electric light post to capture this elevated view of Bournemouth West station on 13 October. 'Battle of Britain' Class 4-6-2 No 34079 *141 Squadron* is backing onto its train to form the 15.09 express to Waterloo.

Right **GUILDFORD:** 'West Country' Class No 34104 *Bere Alston* pauses for water at Guildford with the diverted 10.30 Waterloo to Weymouth service on 10 October.

BOURNEMOUTH: 'Merchant Navy' Class No 35022 *Holland-America Line* towers above its crew – Bournemouth driver Riggs and fireman Savage – at Bournemouth West. It's 15 October and the loco is about to depart for Bournemouth Central and Waterloo. It entered service in October 1948 and was scrapped in May 1966, although its boiler was saved for the future restoration of No 35027 *Port Line*, owned by the East Lancashire Railway.

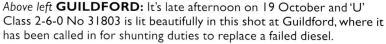

Above left **GUILDFORD:** It's late afternoon on 19 October and 'U' Class 2-6-0 No 31803 is lit beautifully in this shot at Guildford, where it has been called in for shunting duties to replace a failed diesel.

Left **GUILDFORD:** 'Battle of Britain' Class 4-6-2 No 34090 *Sir Eustace Missenden, Southern Railway* makes a stirring appearance on 10 November as it heads the 08.20 Weymouth to Waterloo service, which has been diverted through Guildford due to engineering works. In case you're wondering, Sir Eustace Missenden was a railwayman through and through. Born in 1886, the son of a station master, he started work as a junior clerk on the former South Eastern Railway in 1899, aged just 13! From there he rose through the ranks of the Southern Railway until 1947, when he became the first Chairman of the Railway Executive following the nationalisation of British Railways. He retired in 1951 and died in 1973.

Above **GUILDFORD:** 'Standard 5' 4-6-0 No 73110 waits to work a freight at Guildford Yard. Also pictured are diesel D6549 and No 33027, shunting after the arrival of a local freight off the Portsmouth line.

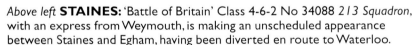

Above left **STAINES:** 'Battle of Britain' Class 4-6-2 No 34088 *213 Squadron*, with an express from Weymouth, is making an unscheduled appearance between Staines and Egham, having been diverted en route to Waterloo.

Above right **READING:** Once a hive of activity and thick with smoke from an assorted roster of steam locomotives, on 27 November Reading South motive power depot is a sorry scene of desolation. The three-road shed had closed in January, and the roof has already been removed; soon the soot-encrusted walls will be demolished too. This view is from the coal road, looking towards the stores. Today an office block stands on the site.

Right **GUILDFORD:** Station pilot 'N' Class No 31411 is detaching vans from the 06.50 passenger train from Reading. In the foreground is 'Tadpole' diesel-electric multiple unit No 1205 ready to depart with a Tonbridge to Reading stopping service.

ROYAL ALBERT BRIDGE: Finally, a wonderful view of the Royal Albert Bridge, spanning the River Tamar between Plymouth on the Devon bank and Saltash on the Cornish bank. Designed by the legendary engineer Isambard Kingdom Brunel – the man behind the Great Western Railway, among other projects – the completed bridge was opened by Prince Albert on 2 May 1859. Brunel died later the same year and his name was placed above the portals at either end of the bridge as a memorial, as can be seen in this photograph. On 30 October 1965 a 'Warship' diesel-hydraulic loco crosses the bridge at the head of 10.30 from Paddington.

Index